1960 to 1969

Social Revolution in the USA

By Rich Linville
ISBN: 9798743383955

The 1960's or Sixties is referred to as a "Social Revolution". It was a time of the Vietnam War, civil rights movements, assassinations, and the beginning of a generation gap. A slogan used during this time was "Flower Power" which was a symbol of passive resistance and nonviolence.

Deep inside Soviet territory and flying more than 13 miles (21km) above the ground, an American U-2 spy plane was shot down by the Soviet Union on May 1, 1960. The pilot, Francis Powers ejected and parachuted to the ground, where he was captured by the Soviets. This caused worldwide embarrassment to the United States and strained relations with the Soviet Union.

In 1960, there were many sit-ins where African American students refused to move from a segregated lunch counter. Many Americans sympathized with the Civil Rights Movement. The Civil Rights Act of 1960 established federal inspection of local voter registration polls and penalties for anyone attempting to obstruct someone's attempt to register to vote or to actually vote.

The Digital Equipment Corporation (DEC) introduced the first minicomputer in 1960 called the PDP-1 (Programmed Data Processor-1). The PDP-1 was the first computer to have digital video games, a text editor, a word processor, an interactive debugger, a chess program, a time-sharing systems and computerized music.

In 1960, John Fitzgerald Kennedy (JFK), a World War 2 hero, was elected president of the United States and Lyndon B. Johnson (LBJ) was elected vice president. The 43-year-old John F. Kennedy became one of the youngest U.S. presidents, as well as the first Roman Catholic to become president. He said, "Ask not what your country can do for you, ask what you can do for your country."

Because Washington D.C. is not part of any state, the 23rd Amendment in 1961 allowed residents to vote finally vote for President and Vice President.
In 1961, the Peace Corps (KORE) was created by President Kennedy for American students to join, help people of other countries, promote a better understanding of the United States, and promote a better understanding of other peoples on the part of Americans.

During the Cold War in 1961, the United States Central Intelligence Agency (CIA) trained Cuban exiles to launch an attack on the Bay of Pigs. It was an attempt to remove the dictator Fidel Castro from power in Cuba. The invasion was a failure and most of the attackers were captured or killed. A United States embargo against Cuba prevented American businesses from conducting trade with Cuba.

The United States Congress said that the Vietnam Era started in 1961 when 900 military advisors landed in Saigon and it ended in 1975. The United States entered the fighting in Vietnam to prevent the spread of communism. North Vietnam was communist and wanted to make North Vietnam and South Vietnam one country.

On May 5, 1961, the first United States human spaceflight was piloted by American astronaut Alan Shepard. It was called Mercury-Redstone 3 or Freedom 7. His mission was a 15-minute spaceflight to demonstrate his ability to withstand the high forces of launching and re-entry. The flight was declared a success.

On May 25, 1961, President Kennedy set a goal of reaching the Moon by the end of the 1960's. He said, "I believe that this nation should commit itself to achieving the goal, before this decade is out, of landing a man on the Moon and returning him safely to the Earth."

On February 20, 1962, the American astronaut John Glenn was the first human to be launched into orbit around the earth and safely returned.

The Cuban Missile Crisis occurred in 1962 when the Soviet Union began to install nuclear missiles in Cuba. The United States refused to allow this and, after thirteen tense days and many secret negotiations, the Soviet Union agreed to remove the missiles.

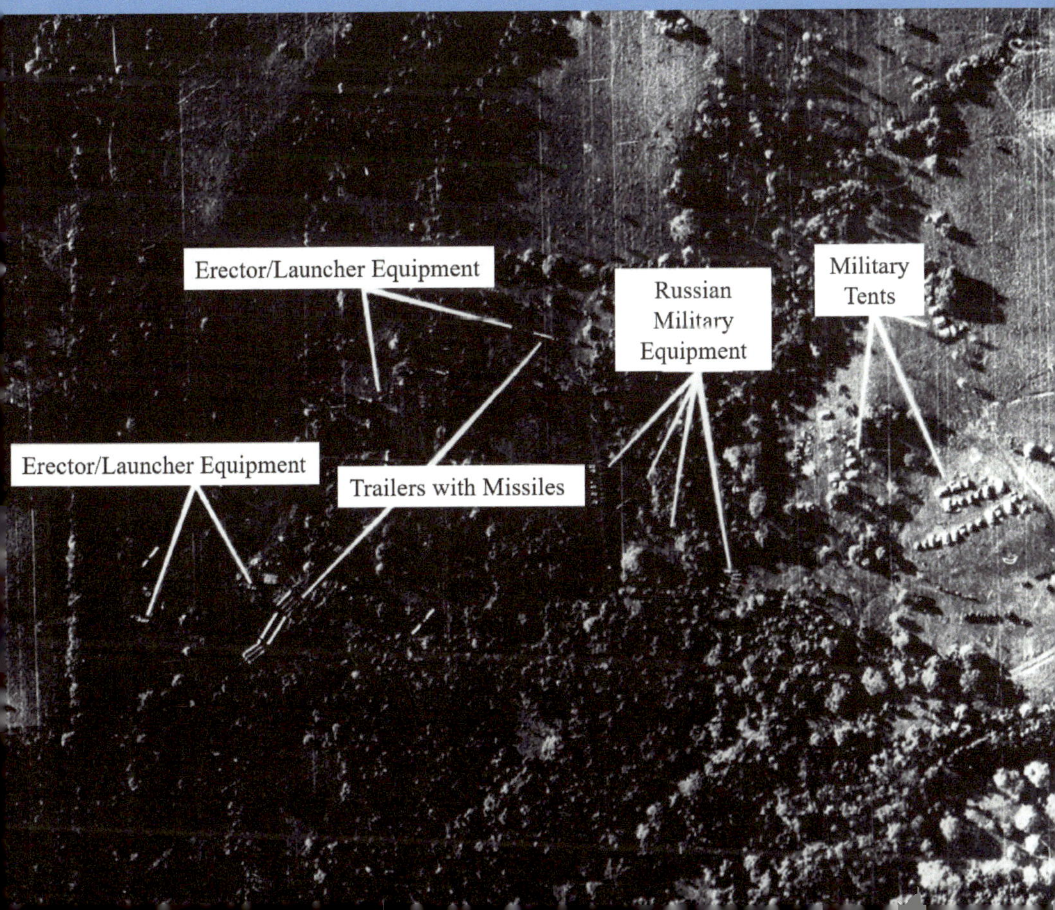

The Cuban Missile Crisis, also known as the October Crisis of 1962, was the closest that the United States and the Soviet Union (USSR) ever came to a nuclear confrontation.

Published on February 19, 1963, the "Feminine Mystique" is a book by Betty Friedan. It is credited with sparking the beginning of second-wave of feminism that said women should have the same rights and the same pay for working that men have.

The United States, Soviet Union, United Kingdom, and other countries signed an agreement called the "1963 Treaty Banning Nuclear Weapon Tests in the Atmosphere, in Outer Space and Under Water". This treaty prohibited all test detonations of nuclear weapons except for those conducted underground.

On August 28, 1963, there was a
March on Washington, DC for
Jobs and Freedom. It advocated
civil and economic rights
for African Americans.

The final speaker was Dr. Martin Luther King Jr., who stood in front of the Lincoln Memorial. He delivered his historic "I Have a Dream" speech in which he called for an end to racism.

On Friday, November 22, 1963 while riding in a presidential motorcade in Dallas, Texas, John Kennedy was shot in the back of the head by former U.S. Marine Lee Harvey Oswald who fired from a nearby building. Kennedy was pronounced dead about 30 minutes after the shooting.

Lee Harvey Oswald was arrested for murder. He denied shooting President Kennedy. Before he could be prosecuted, Oswald was shot dead two days later by Jack Ruby. Still today, some people believe in many different reasons why Kennedy was assassinated.

President Lyndon B. Johnson was Kennedy's successor. Johnson pushed the landmark Civil Rights Act through a bitterly divided Congress by invoking the slain president Kennedy's memory.

Abraham Lincoln/John Kennedy Coincidences and Urban Legends

Coincidences:

Lincoln elected to Congress in 1846. Kennedy elected to Congress in 1946

Lincoln elected President in 1860. Kennedy elected President in 1960.

Both concerned with civil rights.

Both married in their 30's to women in their 20's

Both were succeeded by a president named Johnson.

Both were shot in the head on a Friday in the presence of their wives.

Abraham Lincoln/John Kennedy Coincidences and Urban Legends

Urban Legends:

Kennedy had a secretary named Lincoln, and Lincoln had a secretary named Kennedy.

John Wilkes Booth was born in 1839, and Lee Harvey Oswald was born in 1939.

Booth ran from a theater and was caught in a warehouse, and Oswald ran from a warehouse and was caught in a theater:

Urban legends can be created when some people try to make sense of events in history. It is easy to find seemingly meaningful patterns relating any two people or events. Many urban myths have been proven false.

The Wilderness Act of 1964 was signed into law by President Lyndon B. Johnson. It was established in response to concerns about pollution and protected 9.1 million acres of federal land.

On March 7, 1965, peaceful civil rights demonstrators were attempting to march to the state capital of Montgomery for voting rights. Armed police attacked them in an incident that became known as Bloody Sunday. Televised images of the attack showed horrible images of marchers left bloodied and severely injured.

After the events of the Selma to Montgomery marches the National Voting Rights Act of 1965 was signed into law, by President Lyndon B. Johnson. The Voting Rights Act outlawed voting practices that had prevented African Americans from voting. Martin Luther King Jr., and Rosa Parks attended the signing.

On October 21, 1967, the "March on the Pentagon" wanted to end the Fighting in Vietnam. A demonstrator offered a flower symbolizing "Peace" to military police guarding the Pentagon.

In 1969 Richard Nixon was inaugurated as President. He promised "peace with honor" to end the Vietnam War. Spiro Agnew was Vice-President. Nixon said, "In these difficult years, America has suffered … We cannot learn from one another until we stop shouting at one another, until we speak quietly enough so that our words can be heard as well as our voices."

In June of 1969, the Cuyahoga River caught fire in Ohio. Fires had erupted on the river many times. This river fire spurred legislative action on water pollution control. It resultedg in the Clean Water Act, Great Lakes Water Quality Agreement, and the creation of the federal Environmental Protection Agency (EPA).

In August of 1969, Hurricane Camille hit the U.S. Gulf Coast. It made landfall with 175 mph (280 km/h) winds and caused $1.42 billion in damages. It was the second most intense tropical cyclone on record to strike the United States. The hurricane flattened nearly everything along the coast of the state of Mississippi.

Apollo 11 was a spaceflight that was launched from Cape Kennedy on July 16, 1969. It carried Commander Neil Armstrong, Command Module Pilot Michael Collins and Lunar Module Pilot Edwin "Buzz" Aldrin. Around 650 million people watched the event on television.
APOLLO 11
Michael Collins
Neil Armstrong
Buzz Aldrin

On July 20,1969, Neil Armstrong said as he took his first step on the surface of the moon, "One small step for a man, one giant leap for mankind." With the success of Apollo 11, America had won the Space Race to the Moon against the Soviet Union.

In the late Sixties, the term generation gap was used to describe when the younger generation called baby boomers went against everything their parents had believed in terms of music, values, cultural tastes, and political views

The social revolution of the sixties involved activists who were busy fighting for peace, and racial and social justice as represented in the statue of Abraham Lincoln who said, that we should have "government of the people, by the people, for the people".

The Sixties saw many changes. What did we learn from the Sixties?

Some things that we learned were:

1. Race equality made advancements.

2. Peace promoted the best environment for human potential to flourish.

3. The heroism of humans.

4. A great President like Kennedy made a difference in America.

5. Television can influence people in many ways.

6. Science and Technology made many advances for America.

What else do you think that we can learn from the Sixties?

Dedicated to my lovely wife Sulastri and my grandchildren Mia and Kai as well as everyone who enjoys learning history.

For over 40 years, I have enjoyed teaching at elementary, high school and college levels.

Please follow and check out my author page at Amazon.com/author/richlinville

Illustrations from PixaBay, Wiki, and illustrations purchased from Edu-Clips.com.

Please check out my other books at bookstores and online under the name Rich Linville.

1950 to 1959

The USA's Golden Age Begins

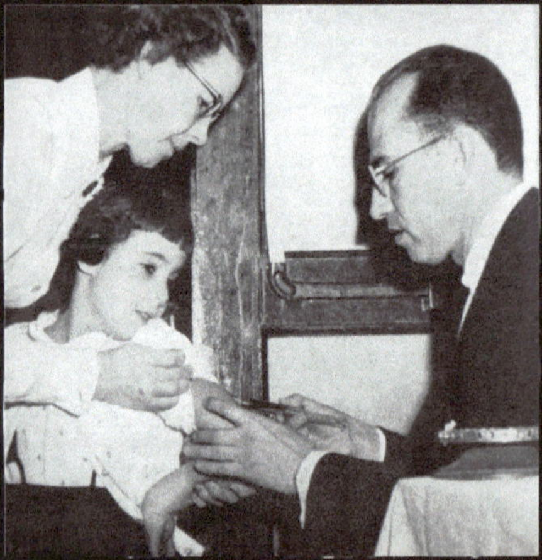

Ancient CHINA

2100 BC to 1912 AD
by Rich Linville

Ancient Egypt
For Kids

50,000 BC to 653 BC

www.ingramcontent.com/pod-product-compliance
Lightning Source LLC
Chambersburg PA
CBHW040929110726
48006CB00001B/120